This Book Belongs To:

· · · · · · · · · · · · · · · · · · · ·

PJJ
I SPY

11/21

Dear Kid...

Do you know how to use I SPY Thanksgiving Book?

Just take this Book to your hands,
Sit together with your Family and Friends,
Open it and play the guessing game,
Look at pictures on the page,
Guess which begin on the given letter,
If you don't know doesn't matter,
turn the page and check the answer,
next time you will play better!

Let's Play

I spy with my little eye, something beginning with...

Congratulations!
You spied !

Letter

is for Ham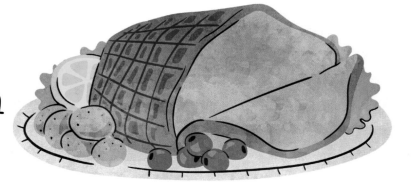

I spy with my little eye, something beginning with...

Congratulations!
You spied !

Letter C

is for Cornucopia

and for Corn

I spy with my little eye, something beginning with...

Congratulations! You spied !

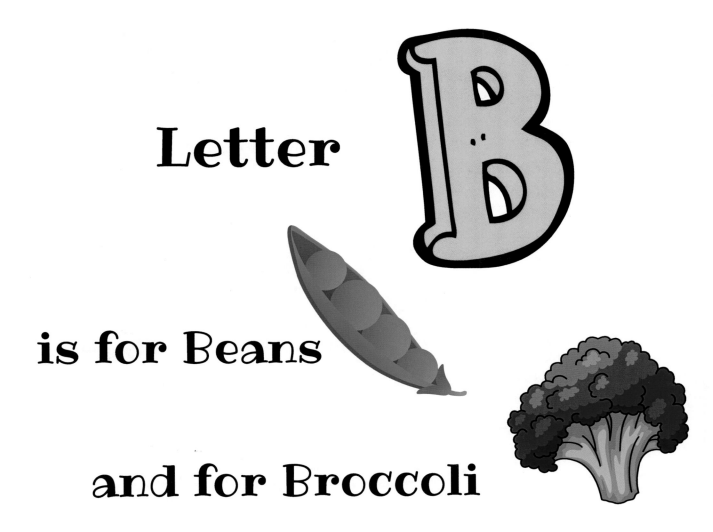

Letter **B**

is for Beans

and for Broccoli

I spy with my little eye, something beginning with...

Congratulations!
You spied !

Letter

is for Gravy

I spy with my little eye, something beginning with...

Congratulations!
You spied !

Letter 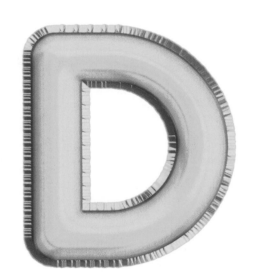 D

is for Dinner

I spy with my little eye, something beginning with...

Congratulations!
You spied !

Letter

is for Apple Pie

I spy with my little eye, something beginning with...

Congratulations!
You spied !

Letter

is for Napkin

I spy with my little eye, something beginning with...

Congratulations! You spied !

Letter

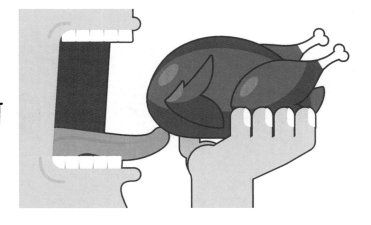 is for Eating

I spy with my little eye, something beginning with...

Congratulations!
You spied !

Letter

is for Family

I spy with my little eye, something beginning with...

Congratulations!
You spied !

Letter

Letter

is for Indian Man

I spy with my little eye, something beginning with...

Congratulations!
You spied !

Letter V

is for Vegetables

I spy with my little eye, something beginning with...

Congratulations!
You spied !

Letter L

is for Leaf

I spy with my little eye, something beginning with...

Congratulations!
You spied !

Letter

is for Platter

and for Pumpkin

I spy with my little eye, something beginning with...

Congratulations!
You spied !

Letter **M**

is for Meat

I spy with my little eye, something beginning with...

Congratulations!
You spied !

T

Letter

is for  THANKSGIVING

Family 🦃 Love Turkey 🦃 Giving 🦃

and for Turkey

I spy with my little eye, something beginning with...

Congratulations!
You spied !

Letter

is for Oven

I spy with my little eye, something beginning with...

Congratulations!
You spied !

Letter  R

is for Rolls

I spy with my little eye, something beginning with...

Congratulations!
You spied !

Letter

is for Wheelbarrow

I spy with my little eye, something beginning with...

Congratulations!
You spied !

Letter **S**

is for Sweet Corn

HAPPY THANKS GIVING

Thanks for reading!

If you enjoyed this book or found it useful
I'd be very grateful if you'd post
a short review on Amazon.
Your support really does make a difference
and I read all the reviews personally
so I can get your feedback
and make this book even better.

Thanks again for your support!

Made in United States
North Haven, CT
31 October 2021